the moment, taken

By the same author:

the moment, taken

jennifer compton

RECENT
WORK
PRESS

the moment, taken
Recent Work Press
Canberra, Australia

Copyright © Jennifer Compton, 2021

ISBN: 9780645009002 (paperback)

 A catalogue record for this
book is available from the
National Library of Australia

Cover image:'Grapefruit and Lace' © Coral Carter, 2017, reproduced with
permission - rubbishphotographer. blogspot.com
Cover design: Recent Work Press
Set by Recent Work Press

recentworkpress.com

SS

Contents

... any other offering ...

... for so many reasons ...

... any other offering ...

the moment, taken

harkening clouds
storming over
our weatherboard house

rolled me tumbledown
with their driven, indifferent
distance

their imperative
going somewhere else
summoned, bidden

then that once, i was waylaid
by a green lure
a staircase

up into a wilderness
within which
each element touched

i sat on a lower step
knees to my chin
nodded, keened

(when i got to school
i told a lie
with eyes averted)

i smashed my head

in a circle before ballet class
hand in hand
with girls in candy floss slippers
and little wraparound skirts

someone wrenched me off kilter
down i went

an odd thwack
it hurt but
i jumped up
differently

i had given my head
a fantastic crack
let something out
let something in

later that night i sat shivering by our fire
odd thoughts were ranging through me
our mother noticed i was
differently
she put me to bed
but

i woke up
to the morning
leaping through the window
differently

ticklish

my sister, with a quirk to her lips

tells me she will never read
a book dedicated to our mother
no way, no wise, no how

as she shrugs herself warm
in a phantasmagorical
three-quarter length jacket

an excess of glitter wool
of mohair, of bouclé, of slub
corresponding buttonholes

she found it in the cupboard
when our mother died
still on the needles

sat herself to complete it
stitch after stitch
wrist and elbow and shoulder

wears it as an everyday thing
while she disavows
any other offering

(i have the non-identical twin
which i wear with irony
it's lumpen, ticklish)

calamine lotion

the first strawberries of the season
returned with a vengeance
blooming on her arms and legs

perfect replicas of their lusciousness
erupting from her flesh
the pink haze of the lotion

drying down to dust
the impregnated cotton ball
her ferocious itch

her fine-pored alabaster covering
the smell of rank honey
in her bending elbow

dainty ginger dots blessing her
so they said
the unexpected redhead

the first one ever to be younger
yowling at the nappy rash
her shit like squashed bananas

my tip-toed attempt to lullaby
she was something of a nuisance
without guile, without finesse

she looked up at the stars
they betrayed her with indifference
twinkle, twinkle

so she took to the cards
the language was arcane
and ticklish

the flare in her green eyes
insane and lucid
she howled on a low note

head thrown back
a thin and plangent
ululation

o darling

a rose, and then another

it's a small knock
like a knuckle tapping twice
on the back of a book

two petals falling
from the singular
flowering

and i am flown
back to that city
and that time

when a particular rose
filched from a midnight garden
(because)

stood in for
so much else, as the heat
(roses are sad in the heat, i wrote)

had laid me dully out on the bed
of the cheapest room i could find
(my unshaven legs)

and the sudden knock
the knock knock knock knock
and knock

of a rose surrendering
all of her petals
in one go

lifted my head from the pillow
what had fallen? what indeed?
and with such a sound

tell a dream ...

my swelling mouth to
your unencumbered
ear

—do you want
to steal
an apple?

day for night
we are on location
the crew intent

about their business
the tree
lit from within

a slick theft
you sly gent
nothing

can be proven
in spite of footage
your legerdemain

—do you always do
everything
as if it is on camera?

you whirl and sting
—stop touching
me

every touch
is like a kiss
every kiss is a nip

like this like this like this!

all the lonely people

i cut my toenails and my fingernails
sitting on the back step in the morning sun

let the clippings fall where they would (like a nomad)
tweezed the menopausal hairs from off my hairy chin

then kicked my heels up as the rock and roll bird
called—*rock and roll! rock and roll!*

once

i found a bat in my raincoat sleeve
my coat is not a habitat

i shook them
(squinched-faced little blighter

give me a fright, would you?)
out into the sunlight

and once, a lizard in my sandshoe
as luck would have it

the lizard squeezed out
of the hole in the toe

a sliver of quicksilver
(i thought my foot was melting)

once a spider fell on my head
a big hairy huntsman

(it was late, i was tired)
a soothing and delicious

swatch of warm velvet
went sliding down my face

the madcap nature goblins

furtively
broadcast
on my ultra frequency
they are jocular
and languid
devil-may-care
in their season
or brisk and down-to-business
vociferous if thirsty
imperious
as a baby squalling in a cradle
as a queen with an agenda
as a rutting stag in full fig
as a dolphin sporting with intent
but they are not animal
no
like i am animal yes
my twitching fingers
my lurching seed-spreading
voracious mobility
i am their creature

flock

one sheep hardly knows
how to eat
alone

the stance to eat
is step and step and step
shoulder to shoulder

the rub
the nudge
the glance

teeth athwart the feed
ravening
within earshot

a clicking, a gnashing
a bustling
a tribal stink rising

and a spooling out
and a looser knot
further, not far

(and a ewe
who has lost her lamb
casts about

mothering a thistle
or
a stone)

plot

each grain slips off each grain
how can i make a garden out of this?

recalcitrant and unrepentant
sullen earth

i need shit, i need worms, and long years
digging in, digging in

until the sudden rain does not glance away
with hurried, scornful panache

like someone not prepared to wait
for a minute, but off

what will grow in such a plot?
nothing much, yet

a jellyfish quilt, shaped like a family

say imagine a patchwork on a daily tide billowing
            gulping
a colony, incapable of loneliness, each for each
            attached

say a fantasia of yesterday's frocks, shirts, pyjamas
            stitched
summon another dimension of fixings and fastenings
            can you?

say she is walking, one foot zigs as the other one zags
            say she sighs
            say she plots
unlatching, surreptitious unbuttoning, working free

her eyes are so innocent that they don't know what her
            hands are doing

it was sudden, it is always sudden

platform 1 flinders street station

the way the people reached and screamed
the way they screamed and reached

a frieze of people on the platform
one arm— and only one— outstretched

a woman shouted—*NO!*
from deep from deep from deep

some decades later—
the adrenaline rush manifests

as a stately parade
of oddball facts

spanning years—
the sound

something between a smash and a crunch
loud, yes, very loud, and mortal

what, and out of the corner of my eye
had that been a flutter or a falling?

a simple second later
i find

i have run sideways
slap up against the brick wall

this is what i do, it seems
to not see

i say— *i am so sorry* to a teenage girl
collapsed into her mother's arms

at the top of the escalator
a stiff-backed silhouette nods at her man

two little lads crimp their fingers
their father kneels and gentles them

and then the sirens
coming from all directions at once

how vivid are the colours of this ordinary day
the coffee and the cigarette are perfect

in the park, a family

he is lying flat
on his face

had a rough week
something like that

she is lying smack
on top

their little kid
doodling about

they don't lift an eyelid
as we walk past

intent upon
flesh, earth

when we walk back
the little kid

is sat
stacks on

the post office, the postmaster

mr grumpy is taking the sun
bum parked on the bike rack

knees akimbo, in vast shorts
face lifted to the empyrean

i drop the lighter that has gone bung
into the bin with a clang

right there, in the doorway
that is where the old guy fell dead

on his morning run
for two papers

no one could get in or out
unless they were prepared to step over

the stretched tarp
few could do that

i think of his non-ambulatory mate
waiting with the kettle hot

how long did he wait before he knew
something was up?

in the museum of the wars

a little man kneeling to sight
along the line of his gun

a little man dying
a little blasted tree

little men advancing
across a glazed sward

little tanks with caterpillar tracks
little planes jinked up on wires

set pieces, in showcases
a stiff procession, behind glass

then—

a black bakelite phone
handy, on the wall

the wooden plaque it is affixed to
smoothed by fingertips

an upright provocation
as my kids and husband mill

i pluck the phone
from the cradle

bend my ear towards
the archival voices

of the tremulous boys
of reverent boys

high, in a bomber
over germany

the lights below blossoming
at their bidding

—did you see that?
—look at that!

they chuckle
drawing in their breath

i did not expect
this blithe parley

in the belly
of the war

then, sudden, a flurry of jargon
pinging through the cabin

and there is a thundering
the noise of the engine

i listen to the loop again
and again

the view from below

cat sitting in brunswick west (on boxing day)

walking today through these streets in this suburb
on the day after the most desolate day of the year
(the withering xmas folderols)

the greek olds gone from the front garden
(the plate of cakes, the diminutive cups of coffee
the thimblefuls of pale fire)

and she is not sitting on the porch in her wheelchair
(her husband perched beside her, nor the dog crouched)
it is the day after that day

the day when your family turned to you their true face
today people keep to the back of the house
musing out of a smeared window

or are howling in thralldom towards a designated camber
one slack fist laid upon the wheel
two cold eyes on the prowl

and I feel, more than ever, that the traffic
is my own worst enemy
the 55 tram from west coburg

is another kettle of fish
i can hear the wheels scream as they lay
into a corner, from the back garden

i can hear the wheels scream
and overhead, a flight path
chopper chopper chopper

the grandson next door of the greek woman
who says she is a 'council worker'
as she cleans the weeds from the roadside gutter

with her back into it, with a twinkle
well the grandson strolls into the outdoor area
at after midnight, even later

pumps up the volume on some hideous game
women screaming, thinly, shrilly
rubber burning, car exhausts

((the little cat has just jumped over my laptop
typed c (for cat?)
then—;kllll))

this all was intended to be about the man
on the frankston train, denatured
by public transport

eloquent about those who flew above him
those who flew overhead
he paced the aisle, engorged and vehement

today, as i was walking, a gangling, solitary man
loped athwart me, on his own path
not a nod in my direction

as if he didn't even notice me
(he didn't even notice me)
tipping his cheap treat

from a sleek, rippable bag
into his mouth
into his appetite

there will be another tragedy

on this new estate built
on marginal land

called something like
mango hill

there is a swell that tilts
the curving streetscape

few trees
few trees

i don't know what mango hill
was called

before it was called mango hill
or what devilment

it holds close
can't overlook

but it looses
unrepentant dogs

from outdoor entertaining areas
to monster us

the first time
a big-chested brute with jaws

made a thrust at a tender child
the woman who held the slipped collar

turning it between her hands
hardly murmured sorry

the second time a woman screamed
—the collar has broken!

an arrogant upstanding dog
went hell for leather

a narrow squeak
home safe

the front door locked shut
and outside the dogs

my own sad, ordinary, human grief

al noor mosque and notre-dame cathedral 2019

it is not beautiful, it is workaday
it is not a soaring exemplar
of our very best

no artisans hewing through centuries
their sins forgiven
and their sons

no gargoyles chuckling and choking
so very like much this one or that
a sly joke for a waterspout

i am not awestruck
by an ineffable kaleidoscope
of coloured glass

this is as simple
as a drink of water
on a friday afternoon

the kind of carpet
underfoot
that can be galvanic

stroke it the wrong way
it will make your hair
stand up on end

our lady of paris is singed
a spire topples

i am unusually grim
during the livestream

the weather in venice

my minder was walking me away from my gig
during which I had casually leant
my antipodean barbarian bum
up against the masterwork of a vast desk
upon which napoleon had signed the treaty with austria

i was surmounting yet another quaint bridge
as the shutters slammed down upon the bars at 9 pm
when the stringent ache in my hip bones
told me it would rain—soon

when I spoke to my companion
she looked twice at me and said
—it is a starlit night

but the next day it rained
it rained. and rained. and rained.

surely this is a fevered imagining

(in 1966 charlton heston was! in new zealand and he did!
play tennis for charity in a closed-off street in wellington)

i am on my way to the central library
on a thin, faraway, long white cloud

so many people in my way on mercer street
a throng

they are all jazzed up and baying
about a tennis match

i am after the books
i push on through

come up against a most unusual creature
a man who is as tall as a tree

in tennis whites
a slazenger in hand

golden hairs upon his legs
a glow of rude health

such planes to his jaw
such luminous teeth

such an unusual colour to his skin
is this what they call a tan?

although he is the very centre
of this circus

he looks lost
he is making

desultory strokes
with his wooden racket

i glance up at him
it is a long way up

he glances down
at the little miss that i am

it was as if he said
—*what is going on?*

it was as if i said
—*you tell me*

i gave him the freeze
and side-stepped him

i am knitting my father a death

for susan

knitting is soothing
as soothing as chooks
bwoork bwoork bwoork

i have been to the shop
bought yarns
chartreuse, vicious lime, magenta

etc
the colours that leapt off the shelf
he is all but blind

we will do the sideways thing
speak as the spirit moves us
or not speak

if there was an open fire
to gaze into
to tend

hours
would go reeling back
summoning

the beskirted heroines
click click clicking
their soft laps

i will ask him to choose
the colour of the day
of visiting

each day a colour
each stitch
a stitch

i will let him scrunch
the rough kiss
of the unravelling

within his hands
as i twitch the thread
away from him

hard at my work
knitting up the scarf
of memory

i shall set the scene

it is silent
my open door lets in a cool pre-dawn breath
my husband is asleep

everyone to the north south east and west of me is asleep
i love them but they have shut up and they are sleeping
i have a cigarette in one hand and a wine in the other

i am thinking about writing poetry
i am not writing it
i am thinking about writing it

there are no bills to be paid
our refrigerator is full of food
my children are asleep, they don't need me

a cool breeze slides in through my open door
i lift the cigarette to my mouth, i lift the glass of wine
and sip

i am the most fortunate person on this earth

i didn't get the studio in paris

BUT i did score a beautiful blouse in a local op shop
that was made in paris
(*BARRAGE* PARIS)

tonight as i sit at my desk wearing it
i come to (almost) fully appreciate the person
who designed it so it just fits great

(with subtle pleats falling from the shoulder line)
and the people who shepherded the fabric
from first thought to bolt of cloth

(that can't be easy)
and the woman who sat at the sewing machine
whizzed the seams together

between (the french equivalent of)
clock-on and home-time
not all of the blouses she made that day were snazzy

i may never get to paris (not in this life)
side-tracked by the stitching (self not contrast)
of the buttonhole on my left wrist

a buttonhole was a big new thought
(self means the same coloured thread
contrast does not)

... for so many reasons ...

Over the Fence

Thinking Of The Call Out For The Anthology For Gallipoli
I Realise I Never Knowingly Met Any Of The Gents Who Were There
But I Knew Plenty Who Were Somewhere Else

So long ago. I was a little piping child.
I don't remember how I got over the fence.
Great-Aunt Mary was mowing the lawn
—*ratchet ratchet ratchet* went the steampunk mower—
and Great-Uncle Frank was collapsed like a marionette,
legs in front (one of them not natural) and bent
to cough and gasp, grey in the face, a misery to himself.
(He was gassed.) (*Dulce et decorum est.*) (Now I twig.)

On this occasion, this one time, before he died young,
he smiled at me. I shimmered up towards him
like a daisy that has learned to walk, and tapped
his unusual leg (trousers rolled up). 'What's this?'
I asked. 'That's where they took away my leg.'
'Why did they do that?' (A curious and trenchant
child.) And then the long, slow, five miles wide
smile of experience.

The One Day of the Year

*'The One Day of the Year' is an Australian play by Alan Seymour
written in 1958 about Anzac Day*

I saw my husband-to-be in this play in New Zealand
when I was 14.
It was on at the Concert Chamber in the Town Hall
and he played Hughie Cook.

As he reached up to turn off the light on his bedside table
so he could pash Jan
I had the strangest thrill.
I wanted a man (him) to reach for the darkness so he could

discover me. (And so he did.)
If it hadn't been for his world-famous programme collection
—'Were you in that play? That was you?'—
years into our marriage

the penny may not have ever dropped.
(The strangest thrill of all.)
As for the play, well
it was about the men who had fought

embodied by men who hadn't.
And I was numbed to the rhetoric
of Anzac Day
how it didn't jibe with the old soldiers

stumbling and inchoate after the Dawn Service
on that one day of the year.
If they could get a grip on
your elbow at the bus stop

—'Don't go today!' Mum would say. 'The men are out!'—
they breathed confusion into your face
the lost boy stark staring
all the words dying on their lips.

The row of medals on their lapel
would clank, would bring them back
and they would unhand you like dropping
something too heavy to hold.

A Farm Near Raetihi

On the shelf beside the brick chimney piece
in the farmhouse lounge room (off the hall)

a room that was out of the usual run of things
(a lofty box, a sash window, a retreating echo)

I came across a copy of *Faces In The Water*
(with a dangerous cover) written by a certain

Janet Frame. A woman by her name, and why
would they lie? And from the words written

on the back, she was one of us. Had I never
laid my hands/eyes upon a book by a NZer

before? (No, never.) I read, sitting on the rump
of a dusty sofa, as the other people were doing

something useful outside. Finding chook eggs
in the orchard, milking the house cow, hoeing

cabbages, rendering horse fat to clean harness.
And the stink of her menstrual blood shook me

out of my orbit. (Forever.) Outside this wooden
box a mountain and her sisters claimed ground.

The Last Time I Saw Dorothy

I had been asked to help wheel her in
to the conference.

We met her at the front of the theatre
as she was man-handled

out of the vehicle.
Those long corridors

with their rick-rack heritage boards.
As I led the way

I heard her gasp at every bump, felt for
her exquisite pain.

So I swung my skirt and stepped out.
Someone has to do it.

As I bent to chock her wheelchair in
I saw her excellent red shoes.

'I see you have your dancing shoes on,
Dorothy.'

Apparently it also hurts to laugh, so
we didn't laugh.

Another View

Landscape and jacaranda
  —Grace Cossington Smith (1933)

Is she sitting?
        Or is she standing?
                In the open air.

No, she is sitting.
        Her eyeline lifts towards
                the flowering.

The sun is behind her
        but I cannot see
                her shadow on the grass.

Time of day is strange.
        It could be almost any time.
                It is overcast.

Within reach of the house
        within which she lived
                the most of her life.

Are there footsteps in the hallway,
        a clattering, a chinking
                in the kitchen?

But she tinkers on. I am imagining
        a foldaway canvas stool.
                A palette.

Today the very day
        the jacaranda begins to slough
                her purple mantle.

Every profligate year
          until it might as well be
                    this year as hereafter.

There the sudden slope of doubt
          that falls away
                    into the unforeseen.

Nothing ever quite comes off,
          nor should it.
                    Mountains looming.

I am standing at the tip of that slope
          looking back at you,
                    Grace.

Take

The photographer's shadow—Olive Cotton (1935)

1

The moment of taking
is the moment she takes.

>He is laid out on the sand.
>He basks in her shadow
>under a monochrome sun.

The triangles of her elbows
are little apertures.

>He almost clasps her breasts.
>His upside down glance
>is telling.

>He (almost) clasps his head.
>He (almost) is an (almost)
>headless torso.

2

Between the wars the shadow falls.
Falls the shadow, as it falls.

3

And then, the parade of young men,
in uniform, with their retinue.
A mother, perhaps a father, a sweetheart,
brothers and sisters, a stoic aunt.
For to have his picture taken
before he is shipped out to the war.
The studio is a clearing station.

(I am imagining this.)

Each young man
glimmering with prescience.
This one won't come home,
laid out upon a foreign field.
(Or beach.)
This one will come home,
but not the same.

4

And then the long years of spring
in the forest. With the returned man.
And then another studio in the town
with her signature above the door.

5

Nothing I am imagining is as true as it was true.

The River Ouse

The Visiting Literary Artist Goes About Her Business

I have an office. (I have a flat also with two bedrooms
and no teaspoons and the carpet is inescapably green.)

I have office hours when students may take advantage
of me. But mostly I bat off emails about how the hours

don't suit, for so many reasons, so I twiddle thumbs like
a person who can no longer smoke in her own office but

has to sit available during her hours, waiting for a knock.
A customer! (A married woman, with a difficult husband,

who I will have to choke off after she has plumbed me for
the grammar and got an A- and taken me out for yum cha.)

She thrusts this piece at me about Virginia striding towards
the River Ouse, quaint dowdy coat, rocks in her pocket yeah!

In this effusion our Beloved tangles with primordial forest
which is looming and glooming, twigs snatching for her hair.

I have an office and in that office I have a computer, so I google
and come upon many, many pics of the banks of the River Ouse.

I turn the screen towards the keen student to show her no forest,
and she does not take it in. It cannot be true. There was a forest.

Two Women

Believe nothing she says. Provide her with a warm coat.
Believe nothing she says. Give her a cigarette, and a light.

Believe nothing she says. When her foot is trapped, stoop,
wrestle with the slab until it yields. Then caress the mark.

Wait for her, wait for her, wait for her two hours before
you give up. Hear out the reasons that she gives with

equanimity. There will be reasons, of course there are.
Believe nothing she says. She isn't lying, you wouldn't

call it lying, but it is an artful art. A kind of inveiglement.
The inconstant narrative of bewilderment. She shivers but

she's not cold, she says. It's winter and we are all cold.
It's cold. But fold away the facts, put them in your pocket.

This is a labyrinth, with a broken thread. Feel about in the
muck, in the dark, for the two frayed ends and make a knot.

It might hold. Or it won't. Beat fists against your forehead.
Confess. You yourself have been dissonant with grief. Why

you write this. Late at night, jangled, without recourse to
irony or impatience or display, at least insofar as that goes.

You yourself would have tried the patience of a saint. So
do anything for her except believe anything that she says.

Tricks of the Trade

The Playwright, In The First Week Of Rehearsal, Makes Herself Plain

'She has beautiful shoulders,' I said. 'And the light pours off
of her skin.'

Because an actor can do anything she took a breath and shone.
But then

all the female actors who had been listening in had beautiful
shoulders

and light pouring off of their skin. I had to rein them in. There
was too

much light bouncing around the rehearsal room. 'No,' I said.
'Just her.'

I know too much about this game but I don't know everything.
Outside

the homeless squatted, in distressed costumes, smoking bumpers,
waiting

in a ragged line for the free lunch. Hunkered deep into their roles.
An apt

tableau. 'Perfect, perfect,' whispered the playwright. 'Don't
change

a thing.' We could smell the free lunch cooking as we clattered
back from

bistros. The downcast eyes took in our feet, but one or two lifted
a glance

with a curious squint, a cool and tilted assessment of the portion
we would

get. Then we were gone, one blink, we were no longer there, we
were voices

ringing from inside the old church hall, emphatic footsteps dancing
to my tune.

Chimpanzee Enclosure

So he said—'Sorry.
We've already invented the space rocket
and the symphony orchestra.
So.' He said.

> a glass cube
> out of the weather
> with 'enrichment'
> tyres on chains
> a gantry of boughs
> titbits stowed
> in unreachable niches
> the makings of tools
> strewn about
> on the cement

Two grown men are stripping twigs
with their meaty hands,
sullenly poking for a 'tasty morsel'
with dumb intent.

They don't appreciate
his comments.
They shrug a shoulder against
his alpha species nonsense.

> a box of glass
> the elements distant
> the green aura
> of growth
> absent
> the tedium
> of scrutiny
> the thud of
> a stranger's
> indifference

It's an uneasy business, staring
through a wall of glass
at our cousins. Impious and
lowering.

'So,' he said. He moved on
to stare at an animal
he would eat
knowingly.

                a young woman
                rushes me
                a deep glance
                through glass
                she entreats with
                an astute gesture
                i am her chance
                but i can't
                she stoops and sits
                close

The Old Man and The Tower

What a knee-buckling
weight he is, the old man
sat astride my shoulders.
The sheer heft of him
the yoke of his thighs
so much meat and bone in him.
A nodding cannonball
for a head, larger than
life-size, his stentor chest.

Homer wrote of Stentor that
his voice was as powerful
as fifty voices of other men.

That loud man died (it is written)
after getting into a shouting match
with the trickster son of Zeus.

Women don't shout, much.
We scream.

*

What manner of tower might it be?
Some crumbling old wreck from antiquity
some grace and favour, heritage-listed
place of last resort for
the faery and the daemon?

Without recourse I carry him
upon the back of my neck
finding each spiral step
with a careful, seeking foot.

Nearly at the top
and still he sings
(like a little child)
hanging on to my ears
(hoping for a good view)
legs dangling athwart.

*

I have the impression that the old man
assumes he is mounting this archaic structure
of his own accord. That each increment
of height seems no more than he deserves.

Is he our sacrifice, will I tip him onto
the cobblestones below once I have gained
the view? Is it a kill-the-father job?
It's like a chess piece, this tower. Crenellated.
Permission to fortify, sir!

This is the territory of answer-back.
This is where the awl of ministry
bites. Enough. Enough. Enough.
Eek eek eek eek eek!

All better now? Calm as a millpond.
Smooth as a smoothing iron
(whatever that is) dashing away.

*

Not one to eschew a burden, no, happy
to pull as hard against the collar or lift
a load as anyone, but my littleness.
Against your immensity.

*

The tower (so it seems) is finite
tops out into vaporous cloud
the realm of what-comes-next.
(There may be other towers about.)
Who knows, I don't know, intent
like a lonely donkey
withers wrung
(a jenny or a hinny)
my being is set upon this task
such is the donkey song.

So I steady you, one hand poised
upon your flank, the other hoisted
on a cant for balance. So and (and)
I take the next step.

The Foundling Wheel

At the Liguria Study Centre in Bogliasco

Karen (a sculptor from New York)
and her boyfriend John
(a fireman)
asked (at table in the Villa of Pines)
if I would like to jaunt along
to the hill town
her grandmother haled from.

(But, odd thing, she would
never dwell upon.
Karen knew nothing
but the name.)

Castle of the Angel
Mountain of Sorrow
(or some such inspiration).

'Can't. No. But thanks.'

(I am already gone and back again
from a slanted chiaroscuro
of an empty square, ticking down
with an almost angry off beat
into the inertia of history.)

(What is already done
is hardly worth doing.)

At table, after, in the Villa of Pines
Karen and John, solemn
told of how the man
with his finger in the books
had waved his other nonchalant hand.

'You'll never know.
This is the name they gave the little one
who fell to earth from nowhere.'

(And so it was that every habitation
had a different name or names
to pick them out, to make it plain
that they belonged to no one.)

It might mean—Abandoned.
It might mean—Found.
It might mean—Unknown.
It might mean—Innocent.
It might mean—Jasmine.
It might mean—Luck.
It might mean—God wanted like this.

'The wheel,' I said.
'The wheel,' I breathed.
I knew about the wheel.

It swung out from the convent wall
and you kissed the baby, once, twice
and then again

or quickly, quickly as you could
knocking an elbow or a tiny foot
thrust it into the depths

(maybe a hopeful token
tucked into the cleft
of a shawl, some left
such a sign)

and swung it to, swung it away from you
swung it shut.

And then, in so short a while
an email from New York
about how John
(a fireman)
had died of an insult to his lungs.

He had ranged the ruins
and breathed the air
of that inimical time.

The time
the towers fell
again and again and again.

The Weeping Man

The night that anchors
        appeared on rooftops
               without makeup
                       in broad daylight.
Fumbling their earpieces
        casting rumpled glances
               over their shoulders
                       at two slim towers.
My son had woken me
        in our night, their daylight
               gently shaken me awake
                       because, America.
My husband was a hired voice.
        We had a top of the range microphone
               in our front room.
                       I waited for the call.
A young man rang before dawn.
        I had been imagining
               who might call. I knew that
                     somebody would call.
And it was him.
        Lifted out of his bed
               he had driven across
                   a darkling city
to speak to me.
        I was offhand.
               'Yes, I know,' I said.
                   'I'll wake him up,' I said.
The husband revoiced almost everything
        in his pyjamas.
               They replaced *Air Force One*
               with *Priscilla*

for instance.

        Did you know that?

                Only a handful know that

                        and I am one of them.

What I remember most.

        The weeping man.

                The purest chance

                        had saved him

from the 101st 102nd 103rd 104th 105th floors.

        The camera was inordinately still

                as he wept and wept and wept

                        and wept some more

dashing rivers from his cheeks

        with his fists.

  `

                A man in a suit, weeping.

                    He made vows.

And then we never saw him again.

        The footage never surfaced

                again.

                        But I remember him.

In Liz and Phil's Garden

It's going to be a good year for pohutukawa.
The buds are fat and bursting.

Liz says round about the second week in December.
Every year at almost the same time.

(I am not going to talk about recent events.
Not at all.)

(Except—the closeup on the screen.
The legend on the passport

of that mother's son
was—'yeux marron'.

Chestnut eyes.
Eyes the colour of the fruit of trees.)

Phil says ... (and now his urgent gesture
is impossible to translate).

Something to do with
(I am not going to mention recent events)

the way we return
penitent

to how seasons
command us.

Such humble, inevitable business.
(Recent events are a world away.)

And now for the resonance of bumblebees
fumbling the rhododendron.

Twenty or thirty hard at it. No bumblebees where
I live now. I had forgotten how unlikely they are.

Intense and unwieldy and furry.
Nobody could make them up.

Traditional and storybook.
Surprisingly nimble at their work.

I tell Liz that writing a lyric
about bumblebees

is a political act.
(In so many ways.)

And a hedgehog, later, that night
ran across the lawn on twinkling feet.

I screamed down the hallway.
'Hedgehog!'

Living its own life
where it lives.

Timeshare in Coolangatta

It just worked out like this. I was up for a few days,
they had a week booked.

The alarum I raised twenty something years ago
is all forgot.

Smoothed, like the incoming tide smooths
the traffic of the sand

twice a day. And the ebbing tide forgets
all over again.

You can't sell a timeshare once you have bought it.
It is yours, while you live, with dues.

They took me round town and they showed me
their best toys.

No, I am not sad.
These are their best toys.

The jingle bells rock of the pokie room,
with a chardonnay sweating on the side,

is a mother and daughter
extravaganza.

They are filling me in on how
the fun works.

They are gazing at me, eloquently,
as if they are hoping I will fall.

(I will never fall.
You can count on this.)

Of course I am sad, as the guardians
of the room strut and fret

dressed in the authority that is brief,
small inducements in their fief.

Downstairs the menfolk are lifting their elbows
as they mainstream sport on the big screen.

I excuse myself and take to the streets.
What else can this town show me?

A solitary bush turkey promenades
as I exclaim about his lonely duty.

To take over the egg mound and to
monitor it—well go, guy!

And a dreadlocked, demented homeless
makes a bed in a shop doorway,

but can't contain himself and springs up
to pace and denounce.

There is so much to denounce. But I wish
for his sake

his whisperers allowed him some leeway.
Allowed him to sleep.

I have a bed that my sister has provided
for me—with an en suite.

But hey—in the dead of night the sister
thunders into my room

and shouts something valkyrie about
where her husband is.

I have an inkling, in my dreaming,
I think he has an early shift.

(I hate this place.
I deeply hate this place.)

The Smoke from Burning Bridges

What did V—do after he had pressed his ultimate Send at 1-49 am?
Weep, pray, rant? Reach for a bottle? Rush into the street? Lie down
on his bed and wank? Choose another likely customer to alienate?
Did his skin stretch tightly across his lonely bones? Did he sweat?
I did not expect it to be the last of him. I thought that he'd reach for
Send again, some chill morning, in his room in the boarding house
on the other side of this city. I made a coffee and went back to work.

*

His ex-wife was wearing vintage leather shoes. His nephew drew breath
to speak a poem he had written that was as near to the truth as anything
I have ever heard. V— monstering the whole house from his crow's nest
at the kitchen table, dropping names like albatross scat. His time-ridden
father, flown in, spoke of his imminent birth. I would have had a private
word with V—, the walnut coffin, the white tulips, in the antechamber
of regrets, but his daughter gripped the lid with her fingertips, and was
pitiful. I withdrew. It was none of mine. After all, I had never loved him.

Late and Soon

Do we love one another enough

                              yet?

Last night I walked down to our supermarket
        through a tunnel of gentle rain
and every person rushing by me was another world
        of difficulty, and difference.

I did not stop them, did not put out a summoning hand
        and mention

                       ice caps.

I allowed their streams of consciousness
        to pass through me.
                Why worry them

                              yet?

Soon enough is soon. If they are not worried

                       now
they will be worried

                       soon.

And if there is nothing to worry about
        we are sweet
                squatting on a mushroom
                    that won't go

                       boom.

A mushroom that goes boom
        is an olden times behind-the-eyes

                       nightmare.

All this time
   I have been pondering
      the wrong storm.

Ha ha ha ha ha

            ha ha.

Three Instances

I am already forgiven
　　　　(over and over again).

There is nothing to regret.
　　　　(When I am thinning radish

I munch the thinnings up
　　　　in all their dirt.)

(I like a bit of dirt, now and then.)
　　　　Knock me off my perch.

It is disgusting to hear me braying
　　　　like a proud fool.

I disgust myself.

*

I sit in my front garden
　　　　like an old woman,

my hands loose
　　　　in my skirted lap,

and I feel the weight
　　　　of my destiny

lift off me.

*

A blackbird in silhouette
　　　　with one golden eye

perched in the leafless
       persimmon tree.

(We all know that particular tree
       dangles golden fruit

from a leafless branch, don't we?)
       (We do now.)

Sudden. So perfect. Mind's eye.
       (I am loved.)

One golden eye, and below
       golden fruit upon the bough.

We All Go Together

Goodbye
            little fidget sipper
                    licking the corner of my eye
                            after my tears.

Goodbye
            six-legged itch
                    hunkered in my hairy bush
                            your covert grip.

Goodbye
            yonder airy leaper
                    the *clip clip* of your feet
                            taken me for a feast.

Goodbye
            the writhe white slim thing
                    ejected from my anus
                            translucent, protesting.

Goodbye
            the busy intimation
                    of habitation
                            of the follicle.

Goodbye
            to the liminal shout of glee
                    as I lay down to sleep
                          they crawl towards my heat.

Afterword

take 1

the moment, taken falls into two parts (in a sense it breaks its back and begins again) the first part ... *any other offering* ... eschews the privilege of capital letters and with an egalitarian spirit moves from the perturbing gift to the gift of the loss in later life

Take 2

The second part ... *there will be reasons* ... begins at the beginning all over again, and picks up the burden of formal written language. With good grace it attends to the rituals of punctuation, that precise craft, and travels from recovered memory to hysteria – and farewell.

Acknowledgements

Antipodes, Australian Poetry Anthology, Australian Poetry Journal, Cicerone Journal, Cordite Poetry Review, Embody, Flash Cove, foam:e, Four W Anthology, Going Down Swinging, Not Very Quiet, Orbis, Poetry New Zealand, Poetry Shelf, Rabbit, Scum Mag, Styluslit, Takahē Magazine, The Best Australian Poems 2017, The Blue Nib, The Canberra Times, The Frogmore Papers, The Moth, The North, To End All Wars, Quadrant, Verity La.

About the Author

Jennifer Compton was born in Wellington (New Zealand) and now lives in Melbourne (Australia). *the moment, taken* is her eleventh book of poetry. Her third book, *Blue,* was shortlisted for the Kenneth Slessor Prize For Poetry; her sixth book, *Barefoot,* was shortlisted for the John Bray Poetry Award; her seventh book, *This City,* won the Kathleen Grattan Award; her tenth book, *Mr Clean & The Junkie,* was longlisted for the Ockham NZ Book Awards. In 2013 her poem, *Now You Shall Know,* won the Newcastle Poetry Prize. She very much appreciates being given the big cheque but she also relishes the hurly burly of the open mic and is an avid performer. So she was delighted to be included in the recent UQP anthology of Spoken Word, *Solid Air.* And delighted in equal measure to have had work selected for *The Best Australian Poetry* in 2003 and 2009, and for *The Best Australian Poems* in 2004 2005 2008 2011 2012 2013 2014 2015 and 2017.

Printed in Australia
Ingram Content Group Australia Pty Ltd
AUHW020931050724
396636AU00002B/9